A YEAR IN THE LIFE

OWL

John Stidworthy/Alan Harris

Silver Burdett Press

Conceived and produced by
Lionheart Books
10 Chelmsford Square
London NW10 3AR

Editor Lionel Bender,
assisted by Madeleine Samuel
Editor, U.S. edition Joanne Fink
Designer Ben White

From an original idea by
Lionel Bender and Dr. J. F. Oates,
Primatologist, Hunter College,
New York

Copyright © Lionheart Books 1987

© 1988–this adaptation
Silver Burdett Press

Adapted and first published in the
United States
in 1988 by Silver Burdett Press,
Morristown, New Jersey

**Library of Congress Cataloging-in-
Publication Data**

Stidworthy, John, 1943-
  Owl.

  (A year in the life)
  Summary: Describes a year in the
life of a North American barn owl as
he catches prey, mates, raises his
young, and survives the harsh winter.
    1. Barn owl--Juvenile literature.
[1. Barn owl. 2. Owls]
I. Harris, Alan, 1957-   ill.   II.Title.
III. Series: Stidworthy, John, 1943-
Year in the life.
QL696.S85S75 1988 598'.97 87-13031
ISBN 0-382-09518-9
ISBN 0-382-09520-0(paperback)

A YEAR IN THE LIFE: OWL
Written by John Stidworthy
Illustrated by Alan Harris

ABOUT THIS BOOK

Our book tells the story of the life of one particular owl over a single year. We have written and illustrated our story as if we had watched the owl's behavior through the year, noticing how its activities changed at different periods. By looking closely at one owl, we give you a good understanding of how an individual animal reacts to others and to the conditions it experiences in the wild.

We have called our owl Titus. On pages 4 and 5 we show you where Titus lives and tell you a little about Titus's habits and lifestyle. Our main story, on pages 6 to 29, follows a year in Titus's life, and is divided up into six sections between one and three months long. Each section begins with a large illustration showing the environment and one aspect of Titus's behavior at that time. The following two pages in each section continue our main story and show some of Titus's other activities during the same period. On page 30 we discuss owl conservation.

INTRODUCTION

There are nearly 140 different species of owl in the world. Owls are easy to recognize. They have a large head, short tail, and a sharp hooked beak with clearly visible round nostrils. Their feet have sharp claws and a strong grasp. They have big forward-facing eyes, set in a face with a disk of feathers. This, and the habit of perching upright, give owls a rather human appearance. But the eyes, beak, feet, and body of the owl are built for a particular way of life. Owls are superbly adapted for hunting at night, though this does not prevent some hunting by day, too.

The barn owl

Our story deals with a barn owl, scientific name *Tyto alba*. Barn and grass owls differ from typical owls (like the tawny owl) in two main ways: the facial disk is especially well-developed and is heart-shaped not round, and the legs are long and look knock-kneed. Barn owls also have exceptionally good hearing.

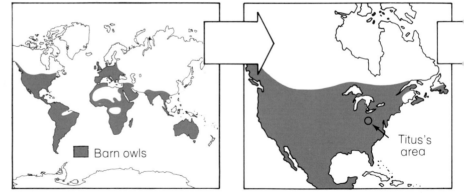

△ Barn owls are found almost worldwide but do not live where the winters are very long and cold. They can be found in prairies, woodlands, tropical forests, and deserts.

△ Barn owls vary slightly in behavior, as well as form, in different regions. Our owl lives south of the Great Lakes, nearly at the north of the barn owl's range in America.

4

Our owl, Titus

Barn owls vary in color and size from place to place. British barn owls are very light in color, with white undersides. Those in continental Europe and much of North America are darker. British owls weigh about 12 ounces.

Our story is about a young male bird, Titus, living in North America, where the heaviest individuals may weigh more than 21 ounces. Female barn owls are larger than the males.

The seasons

In northern America, and in Europe, the seasons are very different. The summer is warm, with trees in leaf, and food is abundant. In autumn it is cool; the trees shed their leaves and the landscape becomes bleaker. During winter and the early spring months it may be extremely cold and food is scarce. Then owls have a hard time. When there is plenty of food, barn owls may rear more than one brood in a year.

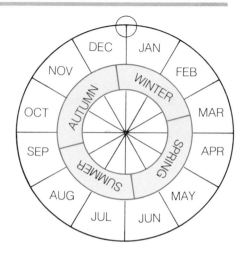

△ The calendar in Titus's range. A small calendar is used in the book to show the time span of each section.

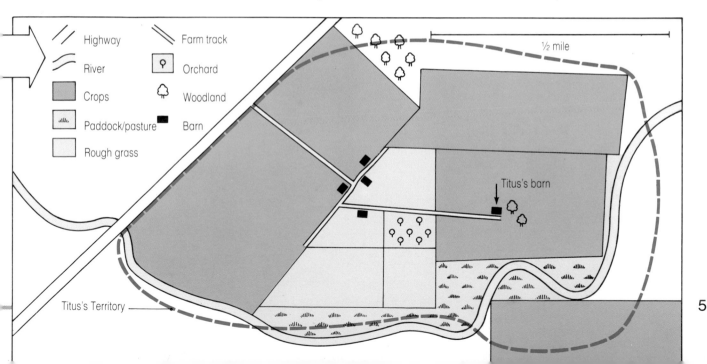

5

OUT AT NIGHT

Titus launched himself into the air and flew silently away from the barn. It was the middle of winter and the nights were long. Darkness had fallen a few hours before, but Titus had not hurried to leave his roosting place and go hunting in the cold night air.

Titus was a young owl, hatched only the year before in a nest more than thirty miles away. Like many young owls, he had not been able to find a living space close to his birthplace. He had kept moving on until he found somewhere not already taken by other owls. He had found a roost in an old barn. Some of the wooden slats making the barn walls were broken or missing. Titus had found a hole at one end, up by the roof, that he used as an entrance. He had his favorite perches on the rafters and ledges. The barn roof was still whole, and Titus had good protection from the rain and the wind.

Outside the barn was Titus's hunting area. Much of the land was given over to crops, but there was an old orchard and some fields of grass that were better for hunting. Best of all was an area of rough grassland down by a small river. This was home to rats, mice, voles, and shrews that Titus could hunt. All winter he had hardly seen another barn owl and he had little competition for food. But most of the small animals, like Titus, spent all the time they could in the shelter of their homes. For part of the winter snow covered the ground and made hunting even harder.

△ Sitting on a perch, an alert owl may bob its head up and down, move it from side to side, or even turn it right around. This helps the owl size up an object or judge the distance to it.

Head for hunting

Mostly Titus rested in the barn but rarely slept. Sometimes he would doze and close his eyes but he was always alert to any disturbance. Often he sat staring at the entrance hole or looking around him.

He could see well in daylight, but his large eyes were also able to see at night when other animals could see nothing. Titus's eyes could not move in their sockets. But his neck was very flexible, and he changed his view by moving his whole head.

△ Owls, like many hunting animals, have forward-facing eyes. These help them judge distances when in flight.

▽ An owl's ear openings are under the feathers, behind and below the eyes.

When it was too dark for even Titus to see, he could still find prey. His ears were very sensitive and could pick up the slightest squeak or rustle on the ground below. The dish-shaped spray of feathers on each side of his face helped to focus sounds into his ears. Titus's eyes and ears worked best when what he was interested in was directly in front of him. He was built for finding prey and lining up for an attack on it. Having heard only one or two sounds he would home in on his quarry with deadly accuracy.

8

Strong beak . . .

Titus had a sharp beak with a down-curved tip. At rest it was often partly hidden in fluffed-up feathers, but it could give a very sharp bite. Sometimes Titus killed a vole he had caught by biting at its head. He could also use his beak to tear pieces off his prey as he ate.

. . . and sharp claws

Titus's long pointed claws, though, were his most important weapons. With his powerful grasp he could sink them deep

△ An owl's big wings have extra lifting capacity for carrying prey in flight.

▷ When owls seize prey the outer toe can be swung back to improve the grasp. It is moved more forward for perching.

into prey. The underside of his toes had scaly pads that also gave a good grip. Often he caught and killed prey with claws alone. He carried it back to a perch in one foot, then settled to eat. He swallowed most things whole, but if he caught a bird or something large Titus would eat it a piece at a time.

As the cold winter turned to spring Titus found hunting easier. Each night he flew out of the barn for an hour or so after dusk and worked his way over the ground. He flew low, watching and listening for the telltale signs of prey. This night he spotted a vole. He spread his wings and glided straight to his target, swinging his big feet forward and spreading his claws just before striking. He was so quick and quiet that the vole had no chance of escape.

Sometimes the night was so black that Titus could not see what was happening on the ground. Then he perched on a post or tree and kept still, listening for movements below. When he detected an animal, he moved to strike, but flew slowly and carefully, beating his wings and with claws dangling. He kept his head pointing straight at the sounds until he was so close he knew he could swing his feet forward and hit the prey.

Often Titus caught all he needed in less than an hour. Then he returned to his roost. He spent most of his time perched, doing little.

As he set out from the barn Titus screeched and for the first minutes of his flight he patrolled his territory making loud screeching calls. Any other barn owls that heard him would keep away. But toward the end of winter another barn owl did arrive. Titus first saw it when it looked into the barn one night and then flew off again. Next night he saw it flying through his territory. Unlike the other owls it was not driven away by his calls.

▷▽ Courting barn owls take part in chasing displays, with the male pursuing the female. The pair can fly quite slowly, the male above and behind the female, or they may take part in fast aerobatics. They call loudly. If a female is perched, a male may flutter in front of her, displaying his body and the underside of his wings. The birds also preen each other.

Courting

At first Titus was wary of the new owl, a female larger and heavier than him. She was not afraid, and came quite close. Titus soon lost his fear, and the two began flying together and roosting in the old barn.

When Titus went hunting now he did not always eat what he caught. Sometimes he brought food back to the female. He held it in his beak and offered it to her. She accepted the present and swallowed it. But often the female accompanied Titus on his evening flights. These became wild chases, with Titus twisting and turning as he followed the movements of the female. As they flew Titus shrieked loudly and was answered by wails from the hen bird.

The two birds were ready to nest. Titus found a possible nest site on boards up near the barn roof. He called the female to inspect it using a quiet purring call. She liked the site, showing her approval by rubbing cheeks with Titus, and started to spend most of her time there.

Mating, and feeding the hen

The two birds did not collect any nesting material; the dirt that built up on the boards made a nest of sorts. Eggs were already forming in the hen. One evening Titus came back to the nest with food for her. He gave a twittering call as he offered it. The female took it and then crouched low in the mating position. Titus mounted her and they mated. They repeated this on several nights, a few times each night. Sometimes Titus brought more food than she could eat, and the bodies of the left over small animals littered the nest.

The young are born

After a few days, the female laid the first egg of the clutch. In all she laid four eggs, one at a time at two-day intervals. She sat and incubated them as soon as the first egg was laid so that the chicks hatched one at a time, not together as with most birds.

▷ The white eggs soon get dirty in the barn owl's nest. The usual clutch size is from four to six eggs, laid at two-day intervals, or sometimes longer.

△ Barn owls mate often through spring and summer, not just at the time eggs are laid. This behavior helps keep the pair together. Once eggs are laid the female incubates them and scarcely leaves the nest. The male feeds her.

Thirty-one days after the first egg was laid, the first chick broke out of its eggshell. By the time the last chick hatched, the first one was already a week old and had grown considerably. For the whole of their time in the nest it was possible to see the differences in size and stage of growth of the young.

This was the beginning of a very busy period for Titus. The owlets began to feed when they were a day old, and from then on needed regular supplies of food. The hen owl stayed by the nest, tearing up the prey and feeding small pieces to the little owls at regular intervals. She also cleared away their droppings. Titus had to hunt hard to feed the family, but most nights he still managed to catch all that was needed in less than an hour. Unless the weather was bad, he caught a vole or rat within a few minutes of leaving the barn.

Ten days after the last egg hatched the female started leaving the young for short periods. She joined Titus in providing food for the fast-growing young, each of which needed a couple of small animals a day. When the adults returned with food, the chicks made wheezing, snoring noises to attract attention. The hungrier they were the harder they snored. Although they were different sizes the chicks all got their share of the food. After three weeks all the chicks were able to take a dead animal offered by Titus or their mother and swallow it straight down.

Growing up

When the owlets hatched they were small and helpless. Their eyes were closed and their bodies covered with thin down. The long head and comparatively big beak made them look very different from the adults. They hatched with the help of an "egg-tooth," a knob at the front of the beak. Unlike most birds, the owlets did not lose this until they grew their second coat of down at about two weeks old.

Until the owlets could see, at the age of fourteen days, the hen fed them by leaning over their head with a morsel of food and touching the base of their beak with it. The hungry ones opened their mouths and took the food. A few weeks after they were big enough to swallow prey whole, they learned to use their claws and beak to hold food and tear off pieces of meat.

△▷ When an owlet hatches it is only about 2in long and weighs about .7oz. By five weeks old it may weigh over 1lb. – more than most adults. The owlet has two sets of down before growing adult plumage.

△ Once the owlets are mobile they keep the nest area clean by moving to the edge to defecate. By a month old they are active and busily investigate their surroundings. A returning parent is met with the chicks' snoring calls.

Danger threatens

The barn was a good place for the young owls. Dry and warm, it was also safe from most enemies. Rats lived below, but few climbed to the roofspace. Then one hot day one of the farm cats came into the shade of the barn and heard the owls above. It clambered up to the beams and started to stalk the owls. Luckily the hen bird was with the young and she noticed the cat. She hissed angrily and, facing the cat, flattened herself in front of the chicks. With outspread wings she looked huge and the cat backed away. It went to look for easier pickings.

△ Young owls may defend themselves. They may roll on their back and strike with their talons and beak if provoked, or they may feign death. The full defensive display of an adult deters most attackers.

△ As the owlets get older they give begging displays, as well as snoring, to attract a parent. They crouch down, put their head up and move it from side to side, spread and flutter their wings.

Becoming independent

The cat returned a week later when the chicks were alone, but by that time some of them could put on their own display. They drove the cat away.

Most of the excitement in the owlets' lives was caused by food. They made a lot of noise and scrambled for food brought by their parents. They were getting so large and rough that Titus sometimes hesitated before entering the barn.

FIRST FLIGHT

Nine weeks after hatching, the young owls were strong enough to take their first flight. Even before this they exercised their wings by flapping them. They walked around those parts of the barn they could reach, and sometimes pounced on feathers or sticks they found. In their play they practiced those actions they would need later in their lives.

When Titus returned with food one night, he found that the two oldest owlets were at the entrance he used to the barn. Instead of going in, Titus settled on a branch in a nearby tree.

The young birds saw him and began to call but Titus did not move. The oldest owlet flapped its wings and called again. Then it let go of its perch and tried to fly from the barn. At first it dropped toward the ground, but then it managed to flap its way to the tree where Titus sat. It crash-landed on the branch and nearly toppled off again. Titus had moved away when he saw it coming, but now he returned and fed it. The owlet managed the journey back at the third attempt, and the brood rested together in the barn roof.

By the middle of August all four young owls had taken their first flights. Gradually they ventured away from the nesting barn. By this time Titus and his mate were roosting in a tree some distance from the barn. It was quieter here than surrounded by their lively family. They even began to dodge the young birds as they explored the area with their clumsy flights. The young birds also spent some time on the ground stalking and jumping at small animals. Sometimes they even managed to catch grasshoppers.

Like father, like son

As soon as the young birds were able to fly confidently their parents stopped feeding them. The fledglings weighed much less than they had at one month old. Fat had turned into muscle and feather. Now they had few food reserves left. They must feed or starve. They tried catching prey they saw while flying. But they were not yet accurate and often ended up crashing in the grass. They also attempted stalking on the ground.

One youngster had most success by waiting for prey. Titus was good at this. He would perch on a post over rough grass and watch and listen before

△▷ When it captures prey and alights to eat it, a barn owl often shields the animal by lowering its wings around it. This "mantling" stops the prey from being seen by other owls or predators. Even young owls in the nest may do this.

pouncing. One night, after he had caught his fill with this technique, his place on the post was taken by one of his sons. The youngster was not so efficient, but he still caught plenty of prey. He repeated his success the next night. It became his favorite way of hunting.

The end to family life

Titus and his mate had spent a busy summer raising young. They were no longer in peak condition. Now the pair moved back into the barn roost. They were no longer pleased to see the young. They avoided them or shrieked at them. One evening the hen bird found one of the young owls in a tree near the barn. She screeched at it, then hissed. The young bird swayed uncertainly on the branch, not sure what to do. Suddenly the hen flew at it, buffeting with her wings and striking with her claws. The young bird fled and never returned. Soon all four young had disappeared from the area. They would each establish a territory of their own.

After this, both adults spent much of their time resting in the barn. There was still plenty of food around when they went hunting. Titus moulted his old coat of feathers and a new coat grew. For about a month he looked untidy but after that his plumage was in peak condition again, and he had recovered from the stresses of hunting for a whole family.

△ Owls have very soft plumage. Even the flight feathers, stiff in most birds, have a velvety surface and a fringe along the edges. This deadens the sound of flight allowing silent hunting.

▷ Young owls are usually driven out by their parents. Many of them fail to find a territory, cannot hunt for themselves, and die. Others travel many miles away before settling.

HUNTING HAZARDS

As autumn arrived the days grew colder. Some of the trees changed color and dropped their leaves. At first Titus was not affected much by the changes around him. The numbers of voles and mice were still high after the summer breeding, and he found enough. In fact Titus put on weight. But as winter drew closer, meals became harder to find. Some days Titus emerged well before dusk to begin hunting. If he was hungry, he also looked for food in the fields in the early morning. Unlike the nights, which the owls had to themselves, the daytime held some dangers. Other birds sometimes mobbed Titus. If he stopped on a perch, they would gather around calling and drawing attention to him. One of his worst moments came when a pair of jays attacked him. They had been feeding on the ground when he flew over. With harsh cries they flew up above him, then made repeated dives at him. Twice they actually struck Titus in mid-air. He was so busy watching them that he went too close to the ground and had to land. They kept on harassing him, and Titus was glad to be able to take off and fly quickly back to his roost.

Titus still saw his mate, but they no longer stayed together all the time. Sometimes she roosted away from the barn. But when they met, they were still friendly. They groomed and preened one another. Occasionally they would screech or have short chases as though courting. For much of the time, though, the two owls were living independent lives.

Producing pellets

When Titus was staying at a particular roost the ground below always showed signs that he was around. Owl faeces are rather liquid and there were white splashes everywhere. The more solid indigestible parts of his meals he got rid of in a different way. Some time after a meal, when he had digested the meat, Titus would cough up a pellet of fur and bones, spitting it out of his mouth onto the ground. Each pellet was quite solid and stayed in one piece.

So a layer of pellets built up until broken down by the action of weather and insects. Titus sometimes produced two pellets a day. After a big meal he would produce a pellet before feeding again. In the nest, the young owls had fed and produced pellets more often. Parts of the barn were covered in litter made up of owl pellets.

▷ Owls spend much time grooming themselves. When two birds are friendly, they often preen one another. Even during the winter a pair of owls may show this behavior. Young owls in the nest also groom one another.

△ Barn owl pellets are oval or round, smooth, shiny, and dark grey. They contain fur, feathers, bones, and sometimes the hard skins of insects. You can get a good idea of an owl's diet by studying its pellets.

A change of diet

Titus's usual prey were the voles that ran through the rough grass. Sometimes he caught a rat or mouse near the barn. But one night after he flew in search of voles without success, his sharp eyes spotted another possible meal. In among the twigs of bushes was a flock of small birds asleep. He flew against the bushes, waking the birds and dislodging them. One fell into an open part of a bush, and like lightning Titus seized it then flew away to eat it at leisure.

A near miss

As the weather got colder Titus took longer to catch his food. He used the whole of his territory, not just his favorite hunting grounds. One night he flew along the edge of a road. He could see a long way, but he concentrated so hard on watching the grass that he did not see a car speeding toward him. He saw it only at the last moment and dodged to one side. The driver was as alarmed by the ghostly shape as was Titus by his near miss.

△▷ Barn owls feed chiefly on voles and shrews, which many other meat-eating animals dislike, but also eat small birds, bats, and insects.

▽ Barn owls often do not notice road vehicles, or trains, until it is too late. Many are killed this way. Others hurt themselves on fences and wires.

A HARD WINTER

The onset of winter brought severe conditions. It was icy for weeks without a let-up. Then came snow, and the snowfall was the heaviest for years. When Titus went hunting he flew across a barren landscape where little moved. Those animals that were active stayed in runs beneath the snow most of the time. Hunting was the hardest he had ever known it. When the wind blew he could not hear his quarry, and on the dark cloudy nights he could see very little. Sometimes he did not eat for several days. He began to lose weight.

Eventually Titus gave up going out when the weather was bad. He stayed in the barn, where he did not get so cold or waste energy in flying. Outside on a bad night it was easy to lose much more energy searching for food than could be gained from any meal he might catch. Whenever conditions were less harsh, though, Titus went hunting. But even in moonlight, catching prey was not easy. He had to wait for unwary animals to appear on the surface and grab them before they disappeared down a burrow or under the snow.

Titus was often hungry and he always felt cold, although he puffed out his feathers to make a better coat for keeping warm. When he did this he looked larger than normal. Sometimes he was a little lonely too. He did not see much of his mate now. Occasionally she came to the barn, but she had taken up residence in a hollow in a big old tree at the other end of the territory. This meant that the two birds did not compete much with each other for the scarce food resources.

More and more Titus used the barn as a roost. He had lived there for over a year now and in the depths of that bitter winter he ventured from it no more than was essential. The barn offered the best possible protection from the elements. It was probably this, and his skill as a hunter, that enabled him to survive the cold months. Once or twice he was also lucky in finding meals when he was close to starvation. Yet under his fluffed-up coat he had become very thin.

An unpleasant surprise . . .

Titus's quiet winter was disturbed one day by the arrival of the farmer with sacks on a trailer. The farmer rarely used the barn, but it was so cold he had bought extra fodder for his animals and needed somewhere to store it. When he arrived Titus took fright and hid in a corner.

▷ Feathers provide a bird with insulation by trapping warm air next to the skin. If it is cold, the feathers are raised to trap a thicker layer. In warm weather the owl looks sleeker.

▽ Owls usually hunt away from their roost. When they are hungry, though, they may take food near to home, such as in the barn where they live.

. . . brings good fortune

Titus went unnoticed, and when he saw the tractor leave he came out of his hiding place.

The animal feed the farmer brought was a great help to Titus. Although he could not eat the food in the sacks, it attracted the rats that lived in the barn. They came into the open to feed. Hungry Titus watched the rats from above then swooped on one of them. A rat made a big meal for a hungry owl. From then on Titus was rarely in danger of starvation. Once again he had been lucky.

Another year

The hard winter took its toll. Titus's mate died from the cold.

Eventually the snow and ice melted and disappeared. Spring was coming and Titus would soon be patrolling his territory, ready to breed again. He would mate that year, and in the following two years, with a young female that arrived later that spring.

▽ In a hard winter, many owls die of starvation and cold especially if they have no shelter.

▷ Barn owls can live up to 20 years but few last this long in the wild. Many die in their first autumn or winter. If food is scarce, young owls suffer first.

CONSERVATION

Long ago people helped the barn owl, without realizing it, when they cleared ground for crops. This produced more of the open country that many barn owls prefer for their hunting. Originally barn owls nested in tree holes and in rock crevices. But they rapidly took to roof spaces, church towers, and especially barns. Old farming methods left plenty of grain exposed to attack by rats and mice, the main food of barn owls. In some places people recognized the usefulness of owls as rodent-catchers and they left special holes in grain stores to allow the owls access.

In the 20th century humans have been less than helpful to owls. Farms have been kept cleaner, with less spilled grain and fewer rodents. Open barns have been built instead of warm, dry, stone or wood barns. Old trees with holes have been cut down. There are fewer nesting sites for the birds. Another factor is the use of pesticides which, sprayed onto crops, stay in the bodies of plant-eating animals. When these are eaten by an owl it receives a big dose of the chemicals. They may kill the owl immediately or weaken it so it does not breed properly. Many pesticides are now banned but a lot of damage has been done. Other factors in owl decline include shooting to "protect game," and accidental deaths from collisions with man-made objects. To conserve barn owls we must ensure they are not poisoned or shot, or their nesting places destroyed.

For further details

Useful information about owl conservation can be obtained from The National Audubon Society, 950 Third Ave., N.Y.N.Y. 10022; The National Wildlife Federation, 1412 16th St. N.W., Washington, D.C. 20036; and The International Council for Bird Preservation, Manoment Bird Observatory, Manoment, MA. 02345.

▷ A barn owl with its young. The nest is in the roofspace of an abandoned stone-built grain store.

Photo: Eric & David Hosking/Roger Hosking